My Horsey, My Horsey, My Horsey

EILEEN DISTASIO-CLARK

Copyright © 2024
All Rights Reserved

With Great Love and Appreciation to those who Have and Do Bless My Life

My Family:

Joseph DeStasio Sr. & Miriam Lucille Baragone DeStasio, My Late Parents.

Andrea Jean DeStasio McIntosh, My Older Sister and their Family.

Joseph DeStasio Jr., My Younger and Only Brother and their Family.

Donna Marie DeStasio Wagner, My Younger Sister and their Family.

My Children:

Eileen, Rebekah, Rachel, S. Michael, Jennifer, Sharon, Tara, Stephanie, Apryll, Mikaelah, & M. Trevor and THEIR Families!!

ACKNOWLEDGEMENTS

First and foremost, I express, deeply, my sincere gratitude to our Heavenly Father for blessing me with the gift and talent of writing! I know I could not do what I do without His assistance.

I also want to acknowledge and express gratitude to the members of my birth family—Joseph Sr., Miriam, Andrea, Joseph Junior, and Donna. All the experiences of my childhood years, experiences that taught me so very much and enabled me to reveal my true self to myself, came about through my experiences and relationships with them.

And, of course, it goes without saying, but I will say it anyway: I also want to acknowledge and note my gratitude to my children, Eileen, Rebekah, Rachel, S. Michael, Jennifer, Sharon, Tara, Stephanie, Apryll, Mikaelah, and M. Trevor, and their families! Through multiple things they said to me, over multiple years, I finally came to the realization that

Heavenly Father gave me the gift of writing and opened the doors to these experiences because He knew that by sharing them with others, others could feel His love too.

And He definitely wants us all to know that He, Heavenly Father, Heavenly Mother, and Jehovah truly do loves us!!!

INTRODUCTION

There are sixteen books in this series, which I refer to as *"The Ellie Series."* All of the characters in these stories portray real people from my life. The main characters depict the members of my family: Daddy is my daddy; Mommy is my mommy; Jeannie is my older sister; Junior is my brother; Maria is my younger sister; and Ellie is me. Now, those are not our actual first names, but they do reference us.

The first story in the series presents our Heavenly Father's Plan of Salvation and takes place in the Pre-Earth World. Now, of course, because we all—when we were born—received what is known as The Veil of Forgetfulness, I do not actually remember everything from or about the Pre-Earth World, but I do know about and understand it from much study and worship as a member of The Church of Jesus Christ of Latter-Day Saints, and memories restored to me through the Holy Spirit. So, from this story there is much truth to be learned.

The last story in the series is set in the Post-Mortal World, and presents a depiction of what happens to us after this life. Again, because I have not gone there yet, I cannot say I 'remember' this. But, I have also learned about the Post-Mortal World from much study and worship as a member of The Church of Jesus Christ of Latter-Day Saints.

All of the other stories are based on true events from my life; events that actually occurred when and how they are depicted in these stories. I chose these events because they are among the many occurrences in my life that presented, or revealed that which I already knew without having to be taught, Principles of Eternal Truths.

Also, I chose these events as the settings for my stories because they depict wonderful learning moments from my childhood and adolescent years, lessons that have blessed and benefited me throughout the whole of my life and will forever continue to do so. Also, through these great truths and their consequences in my life, I have been able to share them with many others, whose lives have also been blessed by them.

So, please read and enjoy, then care and share the messages and stories with others!!

Now, there are also a couple of things you can look for:

In each story, the title of the previous story is presented in *italicized* form, the title of the next story is presented in *Capitalized Italicized* form, and the title of the story being read is presented in **emboldened** form.

Also, every story has at least one word that is uncommon or 'created.'

So, as you read, search, find, and have fun!

MY HORSEY! MY HORSEY! MY HORSEY!

Have you ever wondered why there are horses on the earth? Maybe you think it is because when Jesus, and those who helped Him create the earth under Heavenly Father's direction, put all the animals here, they also put the horses with them, just because they were one of the animals that Heavenly Father wanted to have on the earth. If you think that, you are probably right. But, if you ask Ellie, she would tell you that God did put them here because He wanted them here, but she would also tell you that He did that because she asked Him to, because she loved them so much!!!! At least, that is what she told everyone when she was two years old, three years, and four, and quite a few more! In fact, she still does, just not, or maybe, with the same degree of seriosity!

Now, truth be told, that really does not surprise anyone. In fact, most people who know Ellie well enough to really know her, know that Ellie seemed, and seems, to know a lot of things that no one knew how she knew, things she had not been taught, but also could not be dissuaded from believing, especially things about God and all that He does for us. So, it was no surprise to anyone that Ellie truly believed, and believes, that He put horses here, on the earth, because she wanted them here because she loves them so much, and because she asked Him to.

Now, of course, it was, and is, quite obvious that Ellie truly did, and does love horses. Why, even before Ellie could walk or talk, when her family went for rides through the Pennsylvania countryside, Ellie would wiggle and wriggle, bounce and bump, squirm and squiggle every time she saw a horse in a pasture.

But later? Ellie did not even have to see a horse before the excitement burst from her like air from an overblown balloon. All Daddy or Mommy had to do, was say, "Hey, let's go take a ride," and Ellie was off and running to the car, as fast as her tiny little legs could 'gallop.'

Naturally, as soon as Daddy or Mommy opened a car door, she was the first one in the car, but, just as naturally, the last one to sit down. So excited was she to see the horses in the country pastures that she bounced and bumped and wiggled and wriggled from one seat to another, back row, front row, floor, right side, left side, middle, cheeping all the while, "**My horsey! My horsey! My horsey!**"

Mommy had to sit Ellie on her lap to keep her as still as possible for Ellie, which was still not too still. But still, every time she saw a horse, she became so enthused that she nearly bounced and bumped and wiggled and wriggled her way off of Mommy's lap.

Now, perhaps you are asking yourself, 'Why didn't Mommy just buckle Ellie in her car seat?' Well, I will answer that question for you. There were no car seats then. Ellie was a baby, a toddler, a little girl quite some time ago, and things were quite different then than they are now. So, Mommy had to be Ellie's 'car seat,' and she did a good job at it, even though Ellie still wiggled and wriggled!

And of course, that made being Ellie's car seat every bit of a challenging feat for Mommy, especially when they were taking their rides through the Pennsylvania countryside.

In fact, there was one time when Ellie might have thrown herself out of the car window if Mommy had not been the best-ever 'car seat.' Now, again, you are probably wondering how that could be possible. Well, here is the answer to that wonderment.

It was a nice warm late spring day, sometime in May, and Daddy, Mommy, Jeannie, and Ellie were taking a ride through the countryside. It was really beautiful! The grass was tall, thick and green! The trees were blossoming. They were cloaked with leaves, buds, and blooms! The flowers were also blooming beautifully, their scent was pleasingly perfuming the air, and the wind was swaying them back and forth, and forth and back, and back and fo... well, you know what the wind does with the flowers! And of course, since the car windows were open, the Stations were all enjoying the breeze, which felt fantastic! Jeannie, who was five years old, was sitting on the back seat, looking out the window, gleefully enjoying all the beautiful scenery, and was staying pretty still. But Ellie?

Ellie, who was three years old, was, of course, sitting on Mommy's lap, but, just as of course, she was not sitting still. As she held onto the door, where the window rolled down into it, Mommy held onto her. Everything was fine. Sure, Ellie was wiggling and wriggling, bouncing and bumping, squirming and squiggling, but with no more force than usual, until...

The Stations had been out riding around through what seemed like all the countryside in Berks County, for a couple of hours, and it was almost just about the time that Mommy usually started to get dinner ready. So, Daddy made one last turn down a beautiful country lane, a road that would lead them back to the 5th Street Highway, their route home. Naturally, being a country lane in Pennsylvania, they were, as they had been on the whole ride, driving by stately trees, which were swaying with the breeze, beautiful meadows that were decorated with blooming blossoms, and open pastures, in which, of course, there were horses.

So, just as 'naturally-of-course,' as soon as Ellie saw the horses, she became even more animated than she already was and, not only wiggled, wriggled, bounced, bumped, squirmed, and squiggled, but she also pulled herself up with her hands and pushed herself up with her feet. Then, stretching as much as she could, leaning out of the window, and reaching for the horses, she cheeped something that almost, sort of, in a way, kind of, just about sounded like, "**My horsey! My horsey! My horsey!**"

Well, needless to say, but I am saying it anyway, if Mommy had not been the super 'car seat' that she was, Ellie would most certainly have fallen out of the window. But that did not happen because Mommy, faster than a bolt of lightning could touch the earth from the clouds, well, it seemed that fast. Anyway, with sufficient speed to prevent a disaster, Mommy wrapped both her arms around Ellie and pulled her back into the car with a great big 'hug-me' motion, which Ellie happily returned.

So yes, Ellie, actually all the Stations, truly enjoyed their Sunday afternoon rides through the countryside. Daddy always loved to drive the family around, wherever they wanted or needed to go. But he definitely preferred their drives in the country. They were beautiful, peaceful, and interesting.

Mommy also loved their drives through the countryside. To her, it was almost like a vacation. And of course, she loved having Ellie sit on her lap. That made all the rides quite an adventure.

Jeannie's favorite part of their rides was sitting on the back seat by the window. It did not matter to her whether she sat on the driver's side or on the passenger's side, just as long as she could be by the window and the window could be open.

While Ellie very much enjoyed having Mommy as her 'car seat,' that was not her favorite part of the ride. It was not the songs that the car sang, either. (Yes, I am referring to the radio, but to Ellie, the car was singing.) It was not the car's motion, which Ellie really liked, nor was it the wind blowing through the window, which Ellie loved! It was when they stopped, no, not at home, but by a pasture.

Daddy would park by the fence; they would all get out of the car, pick some grass, and then go to the fence where the horses had gathered. While Mommy helped Jeannie feed the horses through the bottom two fence rails, Daddy, after sitting Ellie on the top rail, holding onto her of course, would help her give the grass to the horses who stretched their heads over the fence.

Now, Daddy did most of the feeding, because Ellie was too busy doing all of the petting. She liked to snuggle their noses and hug their heads. She liked to comb their manes with her fingers. She liked to just love them!! And as she did, she whispered, as best she could, "**My horsey. My horsey. My horsey.**"

"Ellie," Daddy would say, "these are not your horses. They belong to the people who own this farm." Then, pointing to the house that was always somewhere in view, he would ask, "See that house?" Ellie would nod her head, indicating that she did, after which, Daddy would tell her, "There are people who live in that house, and these horses are their horses."

Ellie would look at the house, then look at the horses, then look at the house, then look at Daddy, then look at the house, then, while giving the horse in front of her another 'head hug,' she would whisper, as best she could, and with what sounded like true confidence, "**My horsey. My horsey. My horsey.**"

With a loving smile on his face, Daddy would just shake his head and give Ellie a pretty big 'little hug.' In Ellie's mind, or so it appeared to Daddy, and everyone else who knew how much she loved horses, it seemed that she thought every horse on Earth was her horse!

Oh! And it was not just the ones in the pastures. It was every horse, everywhere! Like the ones they would see in parades. Every year, Daddy and Mommy took the family to see all the parade events in Reading, which was right across the Schuylkill River from West Reading, which was where they lived. And in every parade, the Easter Parade, the Memorial Day Parade, the 4th of July Parade, the Labor Day Parade, the Thanksgiving/Christmas Parade, and any other parades that were scheduled, there were always horses! And, because Daddy and Mommy loved to do things that they knew their children would enjoy, and since they knew how much Ellie loved horses, where there were horses, there were the Stations!

Now, when it came to parades, Ellie did like more than just the horses. For one thing, she loved the music. Why, even before she could see the parade, as she sat on the pavement waiting for it to come her way, she would bounce and bop, shimmy and shake, and wiggle and wriggle to the music that she could hear coming from up the street.

When the parade finally was in front of her, she became clearly excited by the marchers. She stood up and mimicked their every step while pretending to play the drums, the horns, the flutes, the... well, you know, whatever instruments the marchers were playing, she pretended to play them too. She even pretended to twirl a baton. Of course, Daddy and Mommy were very careful to make certain that Ellie did not march off with them.

Oh, and when the floats came by, especially the ones most brightly decorated, Ellie made certain that everyone around her knew how pretty they were. While jumping up and down, she would exclaim with all the excitement a two-year-old, or three-year-old, or four-ye... well, you get the idea, all the excitement she could muster, "Oooo! Blue! Pretty! Pretty! Pretty! (Obviously, Ellie had a special liking for the color blue.) Or, in a not quite as excited, but still very enthusiastic tone, "Ahhh! Red! Nice! Nice! Nice! Or, in a more quiet but still pepped-up tone, "Wow! White! White! White!" Yep, she made certain, with or without intention, that everyone knew how pretty and nice the floats were decorated.

But when the horses came by...

It appeared that at a very young age—about three years old—Ellie already knew that the clop, clop, clop sound on the street was being made by the horses' hoofs. And that was all it took for her to announce, with all the enthusiasm of an entire football stadium on Super Bowl Day, "**My horsey! My horsey! My horsey!**"

Fortunately, Daddy and Mommy knew they were coming before Ellie heard the first clop. That was a really good thing because that made it possible for them to prevent her from running up to the horses, which they knew she would do if she could, by picking her up and holding her until all the horses had passed. And, yes, as each horse passed, she reached out her arms, wanting to give it a 'head hug.'

Oh, and yes, at every State or Local Fair, every festival or community event of any kind, every public holiday celebration, or anything else where horse or pony rides were offered, Daddy and Mommy made certain that Ellie got a ride, or two, or three, or... well, let me just say this; Ellie got to ride and ride and ride. And every time she did, the whole conglomeration of bystanders smiled and chuckled as she announced gleefully, "**My horsey! My horsey! My horsey!**" all the way around the track!!! And, after the ride was done, that same conglomeration of bystanders was heard to sigh sweetly as they watched Ellie give the horse or pony that she had ridden a great big, loving 'head hug.'

Now, you may be wondering, did Ellie really believe every horse was her horse? I mean, really, why would she? Well, it seems that she did, and for the sweetest of all reasons. Since you are probably wondering what that is, I will tell you, and I will also tell how it was discovered.

The Stations, well at least Daddy, Mommy, and Jeannie, liked to end the day relaxing together while watching a television show. Ellie was usually in the living room with them, but rather than watching television, she most often sat on the floor and played with her toys.

However, when they watched "My Friend Flicka" or "Fury," which were shows about horses, or even just a western show, like "The Life and Legend of Wyatt Earp," "Gunsmoke," or "Cheyenne," that had horses in them, Ellie's attention was captured. She would put down her toys, even her favorite ones, and sit, even somewhat still, on the floor, in front of the television, with attention rapt!

Side Note:** For some reasons no one ever seemed to be able to explain, Ellie ALWAYS wanted to sit on the floor, not on the soft, comfy couch, not on the fluffy oversized chair, not snuggled next to Jeannie, not even on Daddy's or Mommy's lap. Nope! Nowhere but the floor! So, the floor was where she sat, directly in front of the television, watching, with rapt attention, the shows? No, not really. She was watching the horses! And, true to her nature, every time she saw a horse on the TV screen, she would announce, in a tone of true conviction, **"My horsey! My horsey! My horsey!**" Now, back to the track.

One night, in early summer, after finishing a delicious dinner of Homemade Pasta with Marinara Sauce, and Tossed Salad, washing, drying, and putting away all of the dishes, helping Jeannie and Ellie with their baths, and assisting Daddy with the last of his tasks for that day, Mommy turned on the TV and, one by one, everyone made their way to the living room. They all settled themselves comfortably in their favorite seats. Well, everyone except Ellie!

Daddy sat down in the comfortable, fluffy, oversized chair. Mommy sat down in the corner of the comfy couch. Jeannie snuggled next to Mommy. But Ellie? Did she sit with Daddy? Nope! Did she snuggle with Mommy? Nope! Did she scoot next to Jeannie? Nope! 'Well, where did she sit?' You may be wondering, or maybe you know, since I already told you, so I will just confirm your suspicion. Yes, Ellie sat herself down on the floor, not the most comfortable place in the living room. Then again, I guess to Ellie, that was comfortable, and it was definitely her favorite place to sit.

Once seated, they all turned their attention to that night's show, which was "My Friend Flicka." After listening to Ellie claim Flicka, and all the other horses she saw in the show, as "My horsey" at least a dozen times, Mommy playfully asked, "Ellie, do you really believe all the horses in the world are yours?"

Ellie turned around, looked at Mommy with an expression that suggested that she could not believe that Mommy had actually asked such a question, and then said, with affirmative emphasis, "Yes!"

"But Ellie," Daddy chimed in, "if they were your horses, don't you think they would live with us? Now, of course, they could not anyway because we do not live on a farm. And, we could not even put them in our backyard because it is too small. Even if it were not too small, since we do not live in the country, and no one can have horses in the city or the boroughs, which is where we live, in a borough, there is no way you could have all those horses, or any horses."

For just a bit of a while, Ellie stared at Daddy. Then, with even more affirmative emphasis, she simply replied, "My horseys! My horseys! My horseys!"

Daddy and Mommy just chuckled. It was quite clear that there would be no changing of Ellie's mind, in which all horses were her horses, no matter where they lived. But Jeannie still wanted to know, and so she asked with curiosity, "Ellie, why do you think they are yours?"

Ellie was quiet. She looked at Jeannie, then at Daddy, then at Mommy, then back at Jeannie. Finally, without saying a word, Ellie got up, trotted across the living room to the stairs, scurried up the steps, and shuffled into Daddy's and Mommy's room.

Daddy and Mommy looked at each other with quizzical expressions. They knew they were both wondering if they needed to wonder what Ellie was doing or if what they thought she was doing was really what she was doing. Now, please note, they really did not have to ask each other what each other was wondering because it was not long before they would see that what they thought she was doing was indeed what she was doing, and did.

After a few quiet moments, they all heard Ellie trot out of Daddy's and Mommy's room. She bounced down the stairs—literally—sitting on her bottom, she bounced from one step to the next and then the next and then the ne... okay, so you know what I mean, until she was on the landing, then she hopped off the bottom step and skipped across the room to where she had been sitting before. She plopped right down on the floor, facing Daddy, Mommy, and Jeannie instead of the TV.

Ellie opened her right hand, and with her left hand, she picked up Daddy's Rosary, holding it by the Cross, she held it up in front of Jeannie. Then, pointing to the image of Jesus, she said, with a quiet expression of gratitude, "He gave me them."

Ellie turned the Cross around and, looking at the image of Jesus with a truly loving expression, she repeated in a whisper as if speaking to herself, "He gave me them."

Jeannie got off the couch and sat down next to Ellie. She sat quietly for a while, then, in a toned that suggested that she really did believe Ellie, she asked, "Why horses?"

Ellie looked up at Jeannie, smiled and in a sweet, quiet voice, said, "'Cause I love them. 'Cause I want them here."

After a few more moments, Jeannie asked Ellie one time more, "But why did He give them to you?"

Ellie looked up at Jeannie, and with a curious expression that suggested that she did not know why Jeannie would even need to ask such a question, she said, "'Cause I asked for them."

Ellie again looked down at the image of Jesus and began to stroke it tenderly, in the same loving way that Daddy and Mommy would rub her back when they held her. As Daddy, Mommy, and Jeannie watched her, they noticed that Ellie was beginning to cry, but not a sad kind of cry, just some quiet tears. Finally, she looked at Jeannie, then at Daddy, then at

Mommy, then back down at the image of Jesus and said, "'Cause He loves me!"

That made everyone smile!

But Mommy was a bit curious about one thing, and because she wanted to know what Ellie would say, she asked, "Ellie, since the horses were here, on Earth, before you were, how did you know you liked horses and when did you ask for them?"

Without looking up, Ellie replied, "I asked for them when I played with them… in Heaven… before I was a baby."

After a small moment, Jeannie gave Ellie a pretty big 'little hug' and scooted next to her. As Ellie and Jeannie sat quietly, looking at the image of Jesus, Daddy got off his fluffy, oversized chair and sat down next to Mommy on the comfy couch. Then, leaning closer to Mommy, he whispered, "She really believes that, doesn't she?"

Mommy was silent for a few more moments, as she continued to watch Jeannie and Ellie. Finally, she replied, also in a whisper, "Yes, I believe she does."

Once again, Daddy and Mommy looked at each other and, without saying a word, they shared with one another the understanding that somehow, in some way that they could not fully identify or even begin to explain, Ellie seemed to know that God really does love us, and just because He loves us, He will bless us with good things and things we love.

Thinking Ellie was too young to understand those things, they had not yet talked to her about them. Still, it seemed that in some miraculous way, Ellie knew things she had never been taught. Daddy wondered what she would say if he asked her how she knew that, but he chose not to ask her because he was pretty sure she would say something like, the Angels told me, referring to the angels she believed sat on the top branches of *The Tree In Their Backyard*.

Now, it was even more evident than ever before, even though it had always been more evident than ever before, that Ellie truly was a spiritual one and that made Daddy and Mommy very, very, ver... well, you know, that made them very pleased!!

Daddy and Mommy snuggled close to one another and, before returning their attention to the TV, watched Jeannie and Ellie 'play' with the Rosary. It was even more apparent than ever it had been, even though it always had been, that Ellie, *Right From The Beginning*, knew that God will bless us with things we love!

After a few more moments, Ellie, hearing Flicka neigh, in one great bound, turned to face the TV and, with hyped up emotion, said, "**My horsey! My horsey! My horsey!**" And, of course, that made everyone smile.

ABOUT THE AUTHOR

Eileen DiStasio-Clark is the second oldest of four children. She is the mother of eleven children and grandmother to twenty-three grandchildren, to date. As a member of The Church of Jesus Christ of Latter-Day Saints, she serves in various positions, teaching, leading, and ministering to children, youth, and adults. Currently, she is also a Family History Missionary. Eileen established the Pursuit of Excellence Institute of Family Education, a non-profit organization focused on strengthening the family. Presently she holds an AA, a BA, and an MA in Clinical Psychology and is working on the completion of her Doctoral Degree.

www.ingramcontent.com/pod-product-compliance
Lightning Source LLC
Chambersburg PA
CBHW042028050526
44107CB00103B/736